demonic tragedy

don't look at me and tell people you know my story,
because you don't.
but then again nobody does.
how are you meant to trust someone with your whole life story?
when you're not sure you trust yourself and your own mind.

sure, i could tell you the story i tell everyone when they meet me,
my name, my age, my occupation,
but don't expect me to tell you about the demons,
that have been controlling my mind when nobody else is looking.

they whisper to me throughout the depths of the night,
and they are part of my story, but i'm not going to tell you that.
questioning everything i do, every move i make,
sometimes i feel as though they could tell you my story,
better than i could.

it's the darkest nights, when it's just me, alone,
that these creatures come into my mind.
"you can't tell people that your drowning in the darkness they'll never
believe you",
they remind me of my true story.

it's a tsunami in my mind,
and the repercussions of this natural disaster include,
loneliness, heartbreak, self-hate,
and the never-ending waves of depression that won't stop hitting,
the shores of my mind.

if you ask the demons nicely, they might be willing to share,
what nobody else knows,
but then maybe you aren't ready,
for the true tragedy,
of listening to my real story.

<u>therapy</u>

"what does it feel like?"
the therapist asks a month after the unexpected tragedy,
her eyes now watching me, trying to unfold the thoughts in my mind,
but i don't know how to answer,
how am i supposed to know how to respond?
when i feel as though my mind is consuming me.

i stop staring at the ground,
but as i look up, i no longer see the therapist in front of me,
but i see you.

it's been happening a lot recently,
where i'm not sure what is my dreams and what is reality,
i lean forward to touch you, to feel your hand in mine,
one last time,
but it's as though you cannot feel me,
desperately trying to reach out to you.
maybe that is how it's going to be,
now you're in a place i cannot get to,
and i'm left behind, here.

"this wasn't meant to happen.
it wasn't supposed to be this way"
i let out, but can anyone hear me?

"it was meant to be a holiday,
you were due to come back after a week,
but the sea decided to take you before that,
and now i am sat waiting for you to come back,
even though i know you'll never be coming home,
to me, to your family, to any of us."
"it's ok" the therapist interrupts.
but it's not is it? how will it ever be ok?

as i get up,
shutting the door to the therapist's office behind me,
i hear my mother's voice echo in my mind,
"therapy will fix it all"
and yet here i am,
feeling more broken than ever

the unknown

why was i here?
here is not where i wanted to be.
i took flowers as most people did,
in a place where colour was at loss.
as the clouds filled every inch of the sky,
the world above me became blurred.
moss coated headstones,
guarding the identity of what lay beneath.
my thoughts caved in on me.
i felt trapped,
like the skeletons that surrounded the earth below.
as i thought, i realised,
unexpected, unforeseeable, unknown lives we live.

masterpiece

you were the worst and best decision that i ever made.
because you taught me so much,
but most of all you made me realise the right choice,
wasn't you.

the first time i met you,
you lay me down with the softest touch,
spread my body out in front of you,
and consumed me.

but i should've known something was wrong,
when you didn't study my body as if it was a masterpiece,
and when you didn't once go to kiss me,
instead you just looked up with desire in your eyes,
because my womanly parts could give you what you yearned for.

why was it that after the first time i didn't realise?
you consumed me time and time again.
but only when you were bored,
and i was vulnerable.
or when we were both intoxicated,
and all that was on my mind was you,
but all that was on your mind was pleasure.

i let you use my body how you pleased,
because you were the first one who touched it,
you claimed it as if it was yours to keep,
and i let you,
because i thought it was me you wanted.

how many other girls were there?
because you can't fool me with the "it is only you" speech,
anymore.
you were a master at this art,
the art of making me feel something real,
when i should have realised all this time it was fake.

the last time i saw you,
i made sure i screamed down the house,
with fake moans and sighs,
to make you think you were in control,

one last time.

oh baby, don't think that you had me fooled,
for the whole three years,
i may have been stupid for the first two,
but this last one i had the control.

i used you to learn,
and you were the best teacher.
you taught me to detect the signs,
for a boy who only wanted to fuck me,
and for that i say thank you.

because i no longer allow anyone of your standard,
to touch the parts between my thighs,
unless they appreciate the stretch marks,
that run up and down my body,
and appreciate how much i have grown.

i will no longer let myself be,
the revolving door for boys like you,
who are so desperate for one thing,
that they don't even appreciate,
the female body for all it has to offer.

so, in the future when you come running back to me,
realising about yourself what i did after two years,
of knowing you,
i will point you in the opposite direction,
and whisper in your ear,
"thanks for being the best and worst decision,
but you should've realised i was a masterpiece from the start"

alone

isolated from the rest of the world,
she stands cold and individual.
the world spins, the people circulate,
yet she remains in that one place.

does anyone notice?
of course they don't.
because that is the feeling of loneliness.
the feeling that hits in waves,
at the most unexpected times.

one moment you're above the line of the water,
feeling as though you can handle the current.
but the next it's like the current is pulling you down,
submerging your head, keeping you trapped and alone.

because how in a world of 7.4 billion,
can one person feeling like they have nobody?
and how is it that the one person can go unnoticed,
as if they were destined to be alone.

she desperately wants someone to notice,
but secretly she wants to disappear.
deep down she's hoping,
for someone to just come near.

<u>travelling</u>

you were half way around the world,
and i was here,
left to my own devices, left with my own thoughts,
alone.
whilst you were exploring,
and doing your thing.
but that left me wondering if i was your thing anymore?
because whilst you were exploring new places,
i was discovering new feelings.
which got me thinking,
does travelling have to be where you go to new countries?
or can travelling simply be the concept of exploring something new,
whether that be about me or about you.

dear past self

dear past self,

i know the world is a scary place, with so much uncertainty hitting every day. But can I tell you something? everything is going to be ok.

i have made it here, to the future. i know you're doing just fine, because i am the person you are going to become.

so please, don't stress.

do not think that the guy who just fucked you over now has the right to make you cry every night, because in a few years he will be the least of your worries. he won't even be worth a look in his direction let alone a teardrop to fall from those piercing brown eyes of yours.

those people who are telling you that 'you are not good enough' please don't listen to them, because really what do they know? just like the guys who will break your heart those people are irrelevant now. you will learn that you are beautiful, and those people are only saying that to you because you are unique and not the same as them.

you are everything that they want to be.

i'm not here saying that your future life is perfect, or that it is everything you expected, because it is not. but you will grow so much, you will have a pure understanding of the world. you will understand that it'll never be perfect but that this life is what you make it. and girl you've made it something for sure.

so, stop your stresses and wipe away those tears, because yes, this life will test you, but you will pass the test with flying colours.

all my love,

your future self.

letting go

i know it's not easy, to let go. but i am here. so please don't feel like letting go is saying goodbye, because i promise that it's not. i will still be here, when you need me. if it's today, tomorrow or five years away, i will be where you left me.

heartbreak

two becomes one.
what was us, is not done.

how could this be?
what did this mean for me?

unknown cries, unknown sighs,
as the spark between us, slowly dies.

everything with us, seemed so grand,
nut then all of sudden it spiralled out of hand.

feelings between us moved to and fro,
neither of us knew which way it would go.

yet here I am, I stand alone,
as I take my first step into the unknown.

turning the page

and so the connection was lost,
just like that, at no cost.
"that's it, i'm done we're through,
i want nothing more to do with you".
you pushed me out and blocked out the aftermath,
you treated me as if, as if i was a psychopath.
how had it got to this stage?
should i sit back and turn this page?
but this wasn't just a page to turn,
this was something of high concern.
at least it was to me,
until you threw away the key.
the key to my heart,
and yet here we are, back at the very start.

this is goodbye

"i best say goodbye" i told myself. i got up and headed towards you for the last time.

but you weren't there. where had you gone?

it was you who covered the extent of my mind. you gave me what no one else did. it was all you. but maybe it wasn't meant to be, maybe fate decided that your time was up. all that is left of you is a memory, my memories, their memories, our memories. but what if... what if... what if that one thing didn't happen. the date is engraved in my mind... it takes me back to that place, between my dreams and reality. two worlds that shouldn't come together and yet i had never needed them to meet more than i did on that day and every day after.

18 years was all it took for you to be called by the mighty man who rules the earth. who does he think he is to take you just like that? i was not ready to say goodbye to you and neither was anyone else. i still see you once a week, in my dreams? in reality? i wish i knew which. i cannot tell if i want to be in your world or mine. for the world, i am in is familiar to me, at least it was until you were taken from it. what is your world like without me? does it feel whole and empty, at the same time?

please answer me.

i sit and wait to hear your answer, but all i hear is my cry. i guess it is time for me to accept that this is goodbye.

<u>my story</u>

i don't need to tell you my story,
its written all over my face,
the events are running circles in my mind,
as though they are part of a race.

eye of the beholder

do you ever think about how you look through someone else's eyes?
you may see yourself as flaw filled,
but to them you could appear as the person you've always wanted to be

<u>heart VS home</u>

home.
is it a place or a person?
do you find it in four walls?
or in a heartbeat made just for you.

the storm

i saw it coming,
it was coming for me.
the storm of chaos,
shook my body and made a home out of my mind.

lost

my feet lead the way,
one foot before the other,
endless steps to a place i do not know.
the places i pass along the way,
places i once knew,
become unfamiliar and untouchable,
as they become blurred,
behind me.
my head fills with thoughts
some of you,
some of me,
some of us.
happy memories leave my mind,
they vanish
and darkness seeps its way in to manipulate me.
my head feels full,
no wait,
it feels empty.
how can i feel both these things at the same time?
worry, loss, sadness, heartbreak.
they drained my body of life,
it was these emotions that had driven my feet to take me,
away from it all.
as i look around it's all black,
overwhelming and unfamiliar,
this is the land of the lost.

seaside

i shut my eyes, yet i know i'm here.
i hear the sea echo forward and back,
like the memories of you, in my mind.

one moment they're clear and close,
the next they're beaten back into the distance,
out of my control.

i see the sand from a distance,
as it tries to desperately absorb the sea,
the way my mind tries to absorb you.

i begin to walk, step by step,
i crave to be close to this landscape,
one that so accurately represents my mind.

as I take a step closer,
the startling sea air pushed me back.
just like you always did.

that's when i realised, it wasn't the sand or sea,
i longingly wanted to feel up close.
instead it was you.

<u>you & i</u>

you and i could have built a kingdom,
we could have had it all,
but instead you left me here,
crumbling in front of the brick wall.

the sun

i wanted to feel nothing,
"go away! go away"
i begged.
but even when i had drawn every curtain,
the sun seeped through the cracks,
and shone a spotlight on me.

that was my saviour,
the moment the sun chose to save me,
from my world of darkness,
and banished the demons who surround me.

<u>the garden</u>

i walk down the garden, its luscious and green,
it's the most beautiful place that i've ever seen.

but my mum walked with me, she gripped my hand tight.
i wondered what i was going to see, that would give me a fright.

although i never did find out, nor did i see,
what it was that my mother saw ahead of me.

head
heart

do you ever get it where your head feels numb
and your heart feels heavy?
and the heaving in your chest and the
silence in your mind scares you?

because i do.

all i hear is the tiny voice in my head,
controlling my brain, my mind and me.
i know my heart longs to be loved again,
to feel something, to feel anything, to feel everything.
and yet all i feel is desperate and empty,
distant and cold.

can you imagine how ironic it is to want to feel
everything all at once, but nothing at the same
time?

because i can.

<u>up & down</u>

i see life as a fairground ride,
always up and down.

you get on half-heartedly,
not knowing what you will encounter.

rush, thrills and excitement,
followed by your stomach dropping.

no matter how many times you go on,
something always takes you by surprise.

it's never an easy ride,
but it'll take you on one hell of a journey.

perspective

let me tell you about feeling alone. you find yourself spiralling down, not being able to get back to the surface. the light is now far above you, with the darkness captivating you and closing in around you. nobody is around you, everyone is gone. you question everything and everyone you left behind, or is it that they left you behind? will you ever escape the darkness? constantly looking forward.

---

let me tell you about feeling content. you find yourself being on cloud nine, higher than you have ever been before, never wanting to come down. light surrounds you, the dark place that captured you is now far behind. everyone is around you, nobody is gone or left behind. you have nothing to question or overthink, only one thing crosses your mind "how did I become so happy and content?" you have escaped the darkness and entered the light. don't ever look back.

mirror mirror

you stand in the mirror 5 years young,
no idea of the future that stands before you.
with every day that passes you are growing.

before you know it, you're looking in the mirror,
at 20 years old. except your mind is not on the future,
but instead your eyes are looking up and down at your reflection,
focussing on the way your thighs touch,
the way your stomach hangs over your underwear,
your growth is at a standstill.

my dear, looking in the mirror,
and emphasising your flaws to yourself will not be your future,
your future look like whatever you desire.

so, stop looking in the mirror.
do not let it determine your future.
do not let it stop your growth.
the mirror does not define you,
but you define what the mirror reflects.

<u>my friend</u>

lost, confused, upset and scared,
i hope you know that i always cared.

you were forever happy, with a smile full of cheer.
but why is it now that you're not here?

one moment i had you, you were there.
and now you're in a place referred to as 'somewhere'.

i'll never again meet someone quite like you.
someone who could fix all that was broken without glue.

i can't explain it.
i can't comprehend.
how it feels to of lost you,
my friend x

<u>me + you</u>

it was you.
you were the maths sum i could never figure out,
the one i could never complete.
i'd spend hours trying to divide up the situation,
each time i'd subtract you or add me,
but nothing seemed to work.
maybe that's because we are inconsistent equations,
we make sense as one,
but together we are impossible to solve.

what they say

do not let what they say stop you from shining bright.
do not let what they say keep you awake at night.

do not let what they say make you sad, upset and cry.
do not let what they say stop you from giving life a try.

do not let what they say define who you are.
do not let what they say lead you to drowning your thoughts in a bar.

life's too short to listen to what they've got to say.
so instead be happy and smile every day!

little world around us

in this world, full of green and blue,
everyone is trying to seek something new.

the wind is forever blowing to and fro.
why it does this? nobody is to know.

is life a mystery? or is life a game?
does everyone in life have the same aim?

who knows if God is even above!
maybe we made it here purely out of love.

whatever this life has planned for us all,
i hope it allows you to be happy and stand tall!

<u>religion</u>

in you i seek belonging.
in you i seek understanding.

lead me through life,
have confidence in me.

take my hand and my soul.
in you i look to have control.

11/10 day of the girl

some of us are poor, some of us are rich,
some of us have to collect out water from a ditch.
but today is the day we become one,
the day we dodge the sexism gun.
for girl, your body belongs to only you.
no one has the power to make it black and blue,
and remember; you have every right to read that book,
without all the men giving you 'the look'.
because girl you have the power if you just believe,
and if someone has a problem, then please ask them to leave.

seaside

i shut my eyes, yet i know i'm here.
i hear the sea echo forward and back,
like the memories of you, in my mind.

one moment they're clear and close,
the next they're beaten back into the distance,
out of my control.

i see the sand from a distance,
as it tries to desperately absorb the sea,
the way my mind tries to absorb you.

i begin to walk, step by step,
i crave to be close to this landscape,
one that so accurately represents my mind.

as i take a step closer,
the startling sea air pushed me back.
just like you always did.

that's when i realised, it wasn't the sand or sea,
i longingly wanted to feel up close.
instead it was you.

so what?

so what if my legs have hair on them?
so what if my stomach hangs over my jeans?
so what if my hair is 'too short'?
so what if my body doesn't fit your expectations?

i am the way i am for me, not for you.
my body is a canvas for me to decorate how i please.

1st VS 3rd

when there is no Wi-Fi we tend to breakdown and cry,
and yet the others in the world will look and wonder why,
because yes, they are crying all the same,
but not because they lost connection in the midst of their Xbox game.
no, they are crying because they're hungry and haven't even eaten,
some are even wondering when they'll next be beaten.

don't you think our problems are pretty ridiculous?
when the others problems, are so conspicuous?
there are worse things happening then breaking a nail,
and getting your clothes parcel a day late in the mail.
yet if it doesn't affect us it's not our problem, right?
because we're all hiding behind our devices from morning til night.

a person cannot help what world they are born in,
but why is it that the 1st world always has to win?
it shouldn't be a competition, nor should it be a race,
based upon the problems we all have to face.
yet maybe next time you go to moan or whine,
think about how the others have it across the borderline.

<u>heart VS home</u>

home.
is it a place or a person?
do you find it in four walls?
or in a heartbeat made just for you.

do they see me?

how do they see me? i sit and i think.
do they really see me? or do they just blink?

i say hello, and i think i look bright.
but do they see the darkness, that lies under the light?

i stand in front of the mirror, i stand and i look.
can people read me like an open book?

do they turn my pages, or do i?
why do they have more control? why? why? why?

i don't think they see me, i don't think they know.
for i am a flower and i will always grow.

they think that they see, and know who i am,
but i cannot be learnt, like the content of an exam.

for i am changing day by day,
i could be on person in September, and another by May.

they think they know me, but deep don't they don't.
so please don't try to figure me out, because i promise that you won't.

__heartbreak__

two becomes one.
what was us, is not done.

how could this be?
what did this mean for me?

unknown cries, unknown sighs,
as the spark between us, slowly dies.

everything with us, seemed so grand,
but then all of sudden it spiralled out of hand.

feelings between us moved to and fro,
neither of us knew which way it would go.

yet here i am, i stand alone,
as i take my first step into the unknown.

the game

everyone is different, no one is the same.
people live life, as though it's just a game.

with every step that you take,
determining the decisions you make.

do i go left? or do i go right?
does anybody know which will help me take flight?

here

you'd tell me that you 'didn't want to be here anymore'.
but where was here?

you'd tell me that here was a 'bad place',
a place where you were no longer needed.
but where was here?

you'd tell me that here was a place for me,
and not for you.
but where was here?

here was a place not just me, but for you.
a place for not one of us but two.

__realisation__

and yet still after all this time,
i look at you wondering why i wasn't good enough.
when really it was you,
who was the one not good enough for me.